D1521187

Super Structures
Burj Khalifa

Dash!
LEVELED READERS
An Imprint of Abdo Zoom • abdopublishing.com

3

Dash!
LEVELED READERS

Level 1 – Beginning
Short and simple sentences with familiar words or patterns for children who are beginning to understand how letters and sounds go together.

Level 2 – Emerging
Longer words and sentences with more complex language patterns for readers who are practicing common words and letter sounds.

Level 3 – Transitional
More developed language and vocabulary for readers who are becoming more independent.

abdopublishing.com

Published by Abdo Zoom, a division of ABDO, P.O. Box 398166, Minneapolis, Minnesota 55439.
Copyright © 2019 by Abdo Consulting Group, Inc. International copyrights reserved in all countries.
No part of this book may be reproduced in any form without written permission from the publisher.
Dash!™ is a trademark and logo of Abdo Zoom.

Printed in the United States of America, North Mankato, Minnesota.
052018
092018

Photo Credits: Alamy, Glow Images, iStock, Shutterstock
Production Contributors: Kenny Abdo, Jennie Forsberg, Grace Hansen, John Hansen
Design Contributors: Dorothy Toth, Neil Klinepier

Library of Congress Control Number: 2017960590

Publisher's Cataloging in Publication Data

Names: Murray, Julie, author.
Title: Burj Khalifa / by Julie Murray.
Description: Minneapolis, Minnesota : Abdo Zoom, 2019. | Series: Super structures |
    Includes online resources and index.
Identifiers: ISBN 9781532123092 (lib.bdg.) | ISBN 9781532124075 (ebook) |
    ISBN 9781532124563 (Read-to-me ebook)
Subjects: LCSH: Burj Khalifa (Dubai, United Arab Emirates)--Juvenile literature. | Skyscrapers--
    Juvenile literature. | Architecture--building design--Juvenile literature. | Structural design--
    Juvenile literature.
Classification: DDC 720.483--dc23

Table of Contents

Burj Khalifa. 4

Building the Burj Khalifa. 8

What Is in the Burj Khalifa? . . 16

More Facts. 22

Glossary 23

Index 24

Online Resources 24

Burj Khalifa

The Burj Khalifa holds the record for the tallest free-standing structure in the world. It towers over the city of Dubai in the United Arab Emirates (UAE).

The **megatall** skyscraper has 163 floors and stands 2,717 feet (828 m) high. A 700-foot (213 m) tall **spire** sits on top of the building.

1

Building the Burj Khalifa

Construction began in January 2004. It took 6 years and cost nearly $1.3 billion to build!

More than 110,000 tons of **concrete** and 192 piles were used in the **foundation**. Each pile was buried more than 164 feet (50 m) into the ground. The foundation had to be very strong to hold the tower.

Around 39,000 tons of reinforcement steel was used to build the tower.

13

The **façade** of the building is made of aluminum, **silicone**, and glass.

The Burj Khalifa has 24,348 windows! Special glass was used to keep the heat out and save energy.

What Is in the Burj Khalifa?

The building holds offices, apartments, restaurants, and hotels. There is also a day care and a grocery store.

An observation deck is on the
124th floor. It has walls of glass
and an outdoor viewing deck.
On a clear day, you can see
for 60 miles (96 km).

The building is home to the world's highest restaurant. It is on the 122nd floor. It also has the world's highest swimming pool on the 76th floor.

More Facts

- It takes three months to wash all the outside windows. A team of people stand on machines that move around the building.

- The building design was inspired by the spider lily plant. Its three wings are based on the flower's petals.

- The Jeddah Tower is in Saudi Arabia. Construction will be completed in the year 2020. Jeddah Tower will be taller than the Burj Khalifa, standing 3,300 feet (1,000 m) tall!

Glossary

concrete – a hard, strong building material.

façade – the front of a building.

foundation – the structure that holds up a building from beneath.

megatall – an extremely large building or structure.

silicone – a hard, dark gray substance that can be used in building materials.

spire – a tall, narrow, upward structure on the outside of a building.

Index

amenities 17, 18, 21

construction 9

cost 9

Dubai 4

floors 6, 18, 21

foundation 11

height 6

materials 11, 12, 14, 15

observation deck 18

records 4, 21

United Arab Emirates 4

windows 15

Online Resources

Booklinks
NONFICTION NETWORK
FREE! ONLINE NONFICTION RESOURCES

To learn more about Burj Khalifa, please visit **abdobooklinks.com**. These links are routinely monitored and updated to provide the most current information available.